3⁹⁵

From Peanuts To President

Photographs courtesy of Charles M. Rafshoon

Library of Congress Number: 76-51267

1 2 3 4 5 6 7 8 9 0 81 80 79 78 77

Printed in the United States of America.

Published by

Raintree Editions
A Division of Raintree Publishers Limited
Milwaukee, Wisconsin 53203

Distributed by

Childrens Press
1224 West Van Buren Street
Chicago, Illinois 60607

Library of Congress Cataloging in Publication Data

Smith, Beatrice S.
  From peanuts to president.

  Summary: A biography of Jimmy Carter, the farm boy
from Georgia, who became the thirty-ninth president of
the United States.
  1. Carter, Jimmy, 1924-   —Juvenile literature.
2. Presidents:—United States—Biography—Juvenile
literature. [Carter, Jimmy, 1924-
2. Presidents] I. Title.
E873.S63   973.926'092'4 [B] [92]   76-51267
ISBN 0-8172-0428-8 lib. bdg.
ISBN 0-8172-0429-6

From Peanuts To President

Beatrice S. Smith

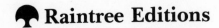 Raintree Editions

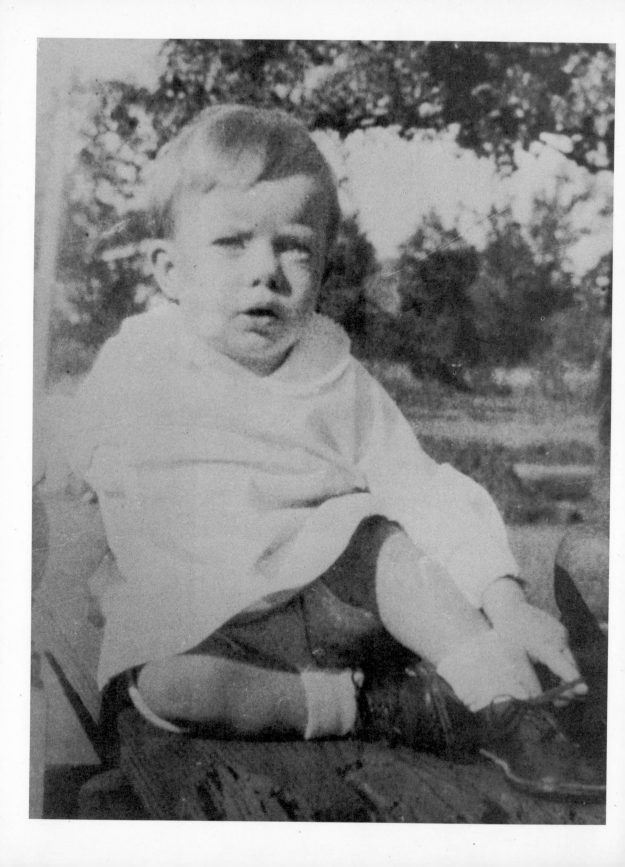

Early Years in Georgia

◀ Jimmy, playing with the laces on his shoe, poses for
his picture at age 2.

It was hot in Georgia that day in 1933. But nine-year-old Jimmy Carter kept walking along the dusty road. It was three miles from his farm home in Sumter County to the town of Plains where Jimmy sold peanuts.

If he sold every bag of peanuts in his wagon, he would make at least a dollar. On Saturdays he sometimes made five times that much, which was more money than many grown men made in a day.

It was hard work. The peanuts had to be picked from the vines, washed, soaked overnight, boiled, and bagged before being carted to town. Selling them wasn't the easiest job in the world either. Often it meant having doors slammed in his face. Sometimes it meant being teased. Once Jimmy was tricked into stepping on a burning cigarette with his bare foot. No matter. Jimmy Carter kept at it. And he didn't complain, especially not to his father. He didn't dare.

Earl Carter, called Mr. Earl by his friends, was strict. The Carter kids were

Jimmy, age 8, leaves for church services with his father and sisters Gloria (left) and Ruth. ▶

switched with a long stick from a peach tree when they misbehaved. Not doing one's job was misbehaving as far as Mr. Earl was concerned.

Everyone in the Carter family worked hard. Their farm had no conveniences in those days. Lanterns had to be filled with kerosene, water had to be pumped, wood had to be chopped, and fires had to be built in the kitchen range. Mr. Earl not only farmed under these conditions, he also ran a supply store and a seed and fertilizer store. Even with all of this work, Mr. Earl found time to take part in community affairs and to teach Sunday school.

Jimmy's mother, called Miss Lillian, was a registered nurse. When on nursing duty, she often worked ten to fifteen hours a day. When not on duty, she helped with the chores, did housework, took care of the children, doctored the sick, and read as many books as she could.

Jimmy's two younger sisters, Ruth and Gloria, also had jobs to do. There were

◀ With the help of his pony, Jimmy, age 10, "rounds up" some of the farm animals.

dishes to wash, beds to make, chickens to feed, beans to pick, sweet potatoes to dig, and a hundred other things. And when Jimmy's little brother, Billy, was old enough, he did his share.

However, life on the Carter farm wasn't all work, especially not for the children. The sun was warm. The creeks were cool and full of catfish. And the trees were just right for climbing, building tree houses, and looking for birds' nests. There was room to run and hide and hunt. There were dogs and horses and mules and kittens galore. And there were always plenty of neighborhood friends around.

A few of the children were white like the Carters. But most were black. Jimmy's best friend for many years was a black boy named A. D. Davis. Jimmy and A. D. played together, ate together, and often slept in the same tree house together. But they did not go to the same school or church. And A. D. did not come in the Carter's front door or sit in their living room.

Jimmy, age 10, carrying a long fishing pole, heads ▶ toward the pond to try his luck.

At the time, these were the rules of the South. They were old rules, dating back to slave days when Sumter County was called "the heart of the Confederacy." Some of the rules were written. Some were not. But everyone understood. And most people, black and white, obeyed them. Jimmy's father obeyed the rules. Jimmy's mother did too — but not always. She tended to the sick, including black people. They were her friends. She respected them and visited them in their homes, and they visited her in her home. A few black people felt free to come in the Carter's front door. When they did, Miss Lillian welcomed them and entertained them in the living room. On such occasions, Mr. Earl would leave the house. White was white, black was black, and each had a place as far as he was concerned.

Naturally, Jimmy tried to please both parents. This wasn't easy. Sometimes it meant changing quickly from one viewpoint to the other. But Jimmy was flexible, and he managed. And when he wanted to "get shut" of it all, he simply took a book and climbed into his tree house. This hideaway was a good place to talk things over with his friend, A. D. Davis.

A. D. and Jimmy did not attend the same school. Jimmy was bused to a school in Plains. A. D. Davis and other black friends went to small schools near their homes. The small schools weren't as good as the one in Plains. But Jimmy didn't think much about that. Not then. He was too involved with his own plans. For Jimmy was a planner — a way-ahead planner.

Navy Life

◀ The members of the Plains High School Class of '41
pose for their graduation picture. Jimmy Carter is in
the front row, far right.

Even before he started first grade, Jimmy and his father talked about his wanting to go to the Naval Academy at Annapolis. When he was older, Jimmy read books about the navy, planned his school work to fit requirements, and studied hard. Sometimes he was teased by more fun-loving classmates. No matter. Jimmy stuck to it.

His biggest worry was that he might not pass the Academy's physical exam. His teeth didn't quite meet. And he had flat feet. There was little he could do about his teeth. But he spent hours rolling his fallen arches over Coke bottles, hoping to correct his flat feet. Finally, in 1942 he received his appointment to Annapolis from a congressman who was a friend of Mr. Earl's.

Jimmy's first year at Annapolis was hard. Freshmen were constantly abused. One punishment was called "shoving out." It meant sitting in a normal position without actually touching the chair. Any show of weakness brought more punishment.

At Annapolis graduation ceremony, Rosalynn and Lillian pin the insignia of rank on Jimmy's uniform. ▶

During World War II, there were dangers, of course. Each summer the naval cadets went on training cruises. German submarines were a constant threat. So were air attacks. Jimmy manned a 4mm anti-aircraft gun battery during the frequent alerts. But he, like the other cadets, also had less exciting duties. Jimmy's job was to clean the toilets. It wasn't pleasant. But he did what he had to do.

When World War II ended, Jimmy was assigned to an old battleship that had been converted into an experimental vessel. Then, after two years, he was given a choice of duty. He chose submarines, one of the most demanding of all possible assignments.

"It seemed to offer the best opportunity for service," he said of his choice.

He also looked forward to working with his boss, Admiral Hyman Rickover. Rickover was tough. He demanded perfection from his men — and he usually got it. No mistakes were allowed. No one got by with excuses. Jimmy expected that. But

◀ Ensign Jimmy Carter (front row, third from left) poses with "O" Division aboard the U.S.S. *Wyoming* in 1947.

he didn't expect to be seasick. At times, Jimmy was so sick he wondered what to do. Should he give up? No. Jimmy was not a quitter.

"He was a gutsy guy," a fellow officer said of Jimmy.

And soon Jimmy was to need all the guts he could muster.

It happened one dark, stormy night south of Midway Island in the Pacific. Jimmy's submarine was on the surface, getting a battery recharge. Jimmy was stationed on the submarine bridge. He was alone. Suddenly a huge wave swept six feet or so above his head and washed him overboard. No one saw it happen.

"I swam for a good while. It seemed forever," Jimmy said of his narrow escape.

Finally, the receding waves landed Jimmy on top of a five-inch gun barrel. He hung on until the water calmed. Then he was able to make it back to his station. Was it worth it? The long hours of study,

Jimmy Carter directs a gun crew aboard a submarine in the South Pacific in 1948.

▶

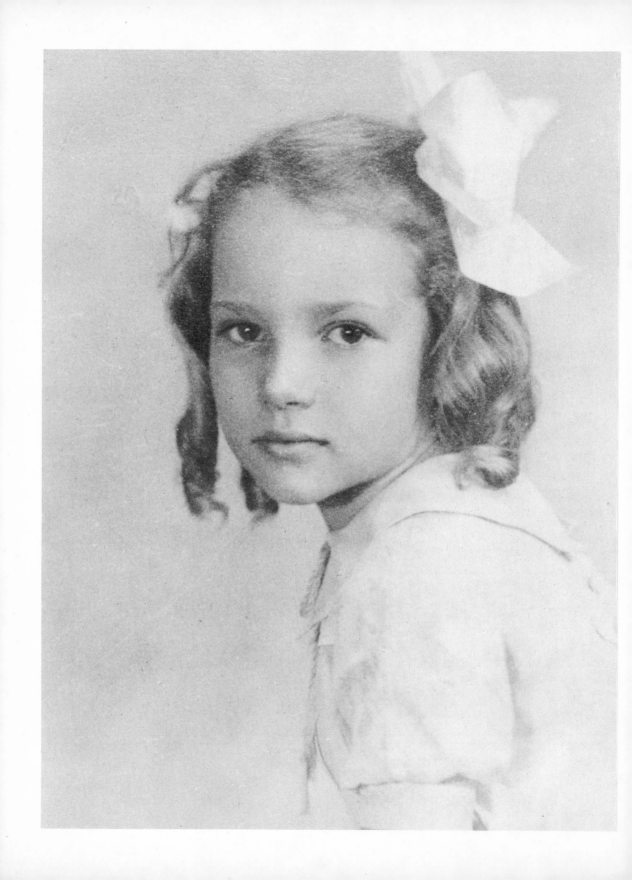

the hard work, dirty jobs, sickness, the near catastrophe? Yes, it was worth it because Jimmy planned to be chief of Naval Operations some day. Chief of Naval Operations? The top job in the navy? "Wasn't this pretty ambitious?" he was asked later.

"Yes," Jimmy admitted. But he always set high goals for himself — and expected to achieve them. Just as he had in Annapolis where the subjects — navigation, engineering, and astronomy — weren't easy. They had left him little time for anything except studying — not even for girls.

But Jimmy had already met quite a few girls. Some were girls he had known all his life. And some he met while visiting his grandmother in Plains. Jimmy's first date, at age 13, was with a girl who had lived next door to Grandma Carter. But he never loved any girl until he met Rosalynn Smith.

Rosalynn lived in Plains and was a friend of his sister Ruth. When Jimmy was in high school, he had seen Rosalynn with Ruth. But she was younger than he,

◀ Rosalynn Smith is poised and pretty at age 10.

and he didn't pay much attention to her. Then, while on leave during his last year at Annapolis, Jimmy asked Rosalynn to a movie.

"Rosalynn's the girl I want to marry," Jimmy told his mother when he returned home that night.

Rosalynn was less sure that Jimmy was the right person for her. But he persisted. Rosalynn and Jimmy were married a month after he graduated from the Academy.

Both Rosalynn and Jimmy enjoyed navy life. They traveled to Trinidad, Nassau, and Jamaica. They saw interesting sights, met interesting people, and learned how other people lived.

Then in 1953 Earl Carter died. It was a sad time even though Jimmy often had been at one end of a switch and his father at the other. He recalled six spankings between the ages of four and fifteen. He got one when he took a penny from the offering plate at Sunday school. He got

Midshipman Jimmy Carter sent this photograph to ▶
Rosalynn in 1945.

Darling I love you with all my soul — got all my life, James

another when he shot a BB gun at his sister's behind. Still, over the years, Jimmy had had only one real disagreement with his father. It had happened when Jimmy was home on leave in 1950. He was describing to his father an incident that happened on a visit to Nassau.

"The whole crew was invited to a party," Jimmy told his father. "But at the last minute we were told that only white members of the crew could attend."

"So?" Mr. Earl raised his eyebrows.

"We had a black sailor in the crew who was really a wonderful guy," Jimmy continued. "So since he couldn't go to the party, none of us went."

Mr. Earl shook his head. He didn't understand. Jimmy argued, softly at first, then more strongly. But there was no way to explain, and nothing he could say would change Mr. Earl's mind.

Though Jimmy disagreed with his father, he loved him, respected him, and

◄ Jimmy's father posed for this photograph in his army uniform in 1917.

longed to be like him. And when Earl Carter died, Jimmy decided to return home and take over the family business.

Rosalynn was upset. Go back to Plains? Go back to small town living, nosy neighbors, bossy mothers, gnat-infested Georgia heat? No. Rosalynn wasn't interested. Not at all.

There were many good things about Georgia, Jimmy argued. They had roots there. Jimmy and Rosalynn had three children now — Jack, Chip, and Jeff. They would have more. Maybe a girl next time. Plains would be a good place for the children. In Plains there were creeks to fish, trees to climb, grandmothers to visit. And, out of the navy, they would be free to do as they pleased. There were old friends to see, new friends to make, not to mention a family business to save.

Then, too, Jimmy told Rosalynn, he had always been interested in public service. Now that he knew a little more about the world, perhaps he could help change it for the better. Whether he could or not, it would be worth trying. She could help.

Rosalynn finally agreed. And in the winter of 1953, Jimmy Carter resigned from the navy and took his family home.

Home Again

Going home was not quite so easy as Jimmy had figured. He and Rosalynn found that they knew little about modern farming. Methods had changed. There was a drought that year. They were badly in need of money and were refused a loan from the local bank.

Jimmy and Rosalynn managed to solve their problems one by one. They learned new farming methods by attending classes, reading books, and listening to advice. Business improved. They didn't need a loan from the bank. They were making it.

Then on June 11, 1963, two black students tried to enroll at the University of Alabama. They weren't allowed to enroll because of their color. They appealed to the Supreme Court of the United States. The Court ruled that all Americans had equal rights under the Constitution — regardless of race, creed, or color. The students had to be admitted, under police protection if necessary.

Ensign Jimmy Carter and his bride, Rosalynn, leave ▶ for their honeymoon.

Both Jimmy and Rosalynn agreed with the Supreme Court ruling. So did some of their relatives and friends. But many did not.

A few who did not agree joined an organization called the White Citizens' Council. Council members did not intend to allow black people into their schools — nor into their churches, nor anywhere else they hadn't been allowed before.

One member of the council was the chief of police in Plains. Another was a Plains railroad agent. The two came to Jimmy and asked him to join. He refused.

"It will hurt your business if you don't," he was warned.

Jimmy shook his head. No matter. "I'll leave Plains if necessary," he replied.

It wasn't necessary. The Carter's business was not seriously hurt in spite of the warning.

But that wasn't the end of it. The Carter family attended the Baptist Church.

Religion was as important a part of their lives as breathing. Besides teaching Sunday school, Jimmy Carter was a deacon. Twelve deacons met and voted on all important church matters. At one meeting the deacons decided that if any black people tried to enter their church, they would be blocked. Unfortunately, Jimmy Carter missed that meeting. But he heard about it.

"It's wrong," he told Rosalynn. "Absolutely wrong."

She agreed. So did his sons and his mother, Miss Lillian. But this was a bad time to cause trouble. Jimmy was now a state senator and hoped to run for higher office. If he wanted the support of his neighbors, it would be smarter to keep his mouth shut.

It would be smarter, but it wouldn't be right, Jimmy decided. The decision made, the Carter family went to church and stood up for what they believed.

A few Plains people were angry. How dare the Carters do such a thing? They were native-born Georgians. Their ancestors went back for six generations. They should know better.

Other Plains people were sympathetic, but thought it foolhardy to stir up a fuss. Still others didn't know what to do.

It was a trying time for everyone, black and white. Habits of a lifetime were being changed overnight. The Carters were having a hard time themselves.

It was 1964. Lillian Carter was running President Lyndon Johnson's headquarters in the county. Johnson backed the equal rights law. So did Miss Lillian. Everyone knew that. And a few hated her for it. Often her car was smeared with paint and her office ransacked.

Chip Carter was 14 years old. He wore a Democratic party button to school one day. The Democrats, under Lyndon Johnson, backed equal rights. Chip had his button torn from his shirt.

Jimmy Carter, successful peanut farmer, proudly
displays an armful of his crop.

Jimmy Carter checked voting records and found election clerks stuffing boxes with illegal ballots favoring candidates who did not believe in equal rights. Jimmy complained to officials. He received letters and phone calls threatening his life.

But gradually feelings began to change in Georgia. Black people and white people had lived side by side for a long time. They had worked together, played together as children, attended each other's weddings and funerals as adults. Both blacks and whites had always obeyed the laws for the most part. Now there were laws that said black people had to be given the same rights and privileges as white people.

In 1966, Jimmy Carter ran for governor of Georgia. In the same year, Miss Lillian, at age 68, joined the Peace Corps and went to India, so she wasn't in Georgia to campaign for Jimmy. However, all the other Carter supporters were there, including many black people. Still, Jimmy lost the election to Lester Maddox by 20,000 votes.

Jimmy was stunned. After trying so hard, working so long — often 18 hours a day — he lost. And the man he lost to was Lester Maddox, the man who chased black people out of his restaurant with ax handles. It didn't seem right.

Right? Who was he to judge what was right? his sister Ruth asked him. God decided such things — not Jimmy Carter.

Ruth's words jarred Jimmy. He had always considered himself a religious person. But was he? For a long time now, he had been overly concerned with personal gains. Winning had become everything to him. What was life all about anyway? Getting ahead? Was that it?

No. Not according to the Bible. People caring about one another was important. Being honest and decent and fair and open was important. Could he be all these things and continue in politics? Yes, Jimmy decided, with God's help he could and would.

Feeling like a new person, he spent much of the following year doing religious

work. Then he returned to politics. With his family and friends, he prayed for guidance, made plans, and worked hard. And in 1971, Jimmy and Rosalynn Carter, their three sons and daughter, Amy, moved into the governor's mansion in Atlanta.

There Governor Jimmy Carter, among other things, began appointing blacks to important positions. He also saw to it that a portrait of a famous black leader from Georgia named Martin Luther King, Jr., was hung in the statehouse. A few white Georgians objected. Most approved.

Five years later a man with a soft voice and big smile held out his hand. "My name is Jimmy Carter. I'm running for president," he told people all across the country.

"Jimmy Who? Running for what?" they asked.

At first even Miss Lillian thought her son was joking.

He wasn't.

◀ Jimmy Carter pauses from his busy schedule as governor of the state of Georgia for a thoughtful moment.

Behind the soft voice and big smile was rock-hard determination. And on November 2, 1976, James Earl Carter, former door-to-door peanut salesman, was elected thirty-ninth president of the United States.

Jimmy Carter, dressed in a tuxedo, smiles as he ▶ listens to voters' questions in his hotel room.

Time Line for Jimmy Carter

◀ One-year-old Jimmy sleeps in his mother's arms.

1924 - Jimmy Carter is born in Plains, Georgia, on October 1.

1935 - Jimmy Carter is baptized in the Plains Baptist Church.

1941-42 - Jimmy Carter is a student at Georgia Southwestern University.

1942-43 - Jimmy Carter attends Georgia Institute of Technology and is a member of ROTC.

1942 - Jimmy Carter receives Annapolis appointment from Congressman Stephen Pace.

1943 - Jimmy Carter begins studies at Annapolis.

1946 - Jimmy Carter marries Rosalynn Smith on July 7.

1947 - Jimmy Carter receives B.S., U.S. Naval Academy; ranks 59th in class of 820.

1947 - John William ("Jack") is born to Rosalynn and Jimmy Carter.

1948 - Jimmy Carter is assigned to submarine U.S.S. *Pomfret*.

1949 - Jimmy Carter is assigned to U.S.S. *Seawolf*.

1950 - James Earl III ("Chip") is born to Rosalynn and Jimmy Carter.

1952 - Jimmy Carter is assigned to Atomic Energy Commission, Division of Reactor Development in Schenectady, New York.

1953 - Jimmy Carter resigns from the navy and returns to Georgia.

1953 - Jimmy Carter refuses to join the White Citizens' Council.

1953 - Donnel Jeffrey ("Jeff") is born to Rosalynn and Jimmy Carter.

1962-66 - Jimmy Carter serves as a member of the Georgia State Senate.

1966 - Jimmy Carter loses gubernatorial race in Georgia.

1968 - Amy Lynn is born to Rosalynn and Jimmy Carter.

1971-74 - Jimmy Carter serves as governor of Georgia.

1976 - Jimmy Carter is elected president of the United States on November 2.